DATE DUE

JA 5 '06			
AP 27 '08			
DE 0 2 '08			
MY 2 0 '09			
MY 0 2 '10			
AG 0 3 '09			
SE 0 7 '10			
SE 0 7 '13			
MR 0 9 '13			

SKATEBOARDING

by Russ Spencer

Content Adviser: Pearl Tesler, Author and Journalist, Exploratorium, San Francisco, California

KIDS' GUIDES SPORTS

Published in the United States of America by The Child's World®
PO Box 326 • Chanhassen, MN 55317-0326 • 800-599-READ • www.childsworld.com

Acknowledgments

The Child's World®: Mary Berendes, Publishing Director

Editorial Directions, Inc.: E. Russell Primm, Editorial Director; Melissa McDaniel, Line Editor; Matt Messbarger, Project Editor and Editorial Assistant; Susan Hindman, Copy Editor; Susan Ashley, Proofreader; Terry Johnson, Olivia Nellums, Katharine Trickle, and Julie Zaveloff, Fact Checkers; Tim Griffin/IndexServ, Indexer; James Buckley Jr. and James Gigliotti, Photo Researchers and Selectors

Editorial and photo research services provided by Shoreline Publishing Group LLC, Santa Barbara, California

The Design Lab: Kathleen Petelinsek, Art Direction and Design; Kari Thornborough, Art Production

Photos

Cover: Duomo/Corbis; Bettmann/Corbis: 8; Stanley Chou/Getty Images: 13; Corbis: 14; Duomo/Corbis: 21; Jason Merritt/WireImage: 25; Rick Rickman/NewSport/Corbis: 28; H. Armstrong Roberts/Corbis: 7; Patty Segovia: 26; Sports Gallery/Al Messerschmidt: 5, 16, 19, 22; Karl Weatherly/Corbis: 11.

Registration

Library of Congress Cataloging-in-Publication Data

Spencer, Russ.
    Skateboarding / by Russ Spencer.
        v. cm. — (Kids' guides)
    Includes bibliographical references (p.   ) and index.
    Contents: Into the great wide open—Gear up!—In action—Stars and competition.
    ISBN 1-59296-210-6 (lib. bdg. : alk. paper) 1. Skateboarding—Juvenile literature.
[1. Skateboarding.] I. Title. II. Series.
    GV859.8.S64 2004
    796.22—dc22   2003027370

CONTENTS

GO RIP!

In the sport of skateboarding, all you

need is a board and the willingness to go out and ride it. You don't need a stadium or a field or a diamond or an umpire. There are no bases, end zones, or fouls. You don't need to live near the ocean or in the mountains. Perhaps most important, there is absolutely no sitting on the bench.

You want to **rip**? Go rip.

In fact, the lack of rules is part of what has made skateboarding so popular with kids since it began in the 1950s. Its popularity has grown steadily over the years, and now more than 11 million people skateboard each year.

Why so many? Because it's an individual expressive sport for everyone. But it's also a sport you can enjoy doing with your friends. You're all playing for the same team—your team. You can walk out your front door and turn your neighborhood into your own personal skate park. And once you've paid for your board, pads, and helmet, it's entirely free. It's a free sport, and you feel free doing it.

Everyone's skating landscape is different. Some people have hills and smooth streets and curbs. Others have flat, rough streets. None of this matters. What matters—like anything else in life—is what you do with what you have. The most success-

Cool clothes and hot moves: skateboarding takes great balance and lots of practice to master.

ful skaters approach the sport creatively. This is what makes skating an art form. You take the landscape you are given and make the most of it.

There's a curb. Are you going to ollie over it? Rail slide it? Grind it? It's up to you. Even if you're lucky enough to have access to a skate park or a **half-pipe,** the props are there only to help spur your creativity. (Don't worry, we'll explain what all those things mean if you don't already know!)

So, express yourself.

Of course, many skating tricks have become famous, such as ollies, **aerials,** nose wheelies, **kick flips,** and more. But the skaters who thought up these moves and made them famous were expressing themselves. They came up with something new. People around them saw it and were impressed and imitated their moves. But it all started with a spark—the spark of inspiration on the part of the original skater. You can do the same thing.

Skateboarding is a sport of freedom. But, like Spider-Man says, with great freedom also comes great responsibility. In 2000, nearly 50,000 children ages 5 to 14 were treated in hospital emergency rooms for skateboarding-related injuries. Also, the sport's reputation has suffered because of skaters who damage public property. The best skaters understand that being safe and following some rules make skating more fun, not less. Be **rad,** but be safe. Have fun, but don't damage other people's property. Get **vert,** but don't get hurt.

Skateboarding was not invented by

adults who thought they knew what kids wanted. Like a lot of

cool things, skateboarding was invented by kids.

Though skateboarding goes back to the early 1900s, it

didn't catch on until the 1950s. Hawaiian and Southern Califor-

nia surfers wanted something to do when there were no waves.

So they did the only sensible thing. They tore apart their little

sisters' roller skates and hammered the steel wheels onto pieces

The first skate-
boarders took
their inspiration
from surfers
such as these.

Skaters have always made skate parks out of unlikely areas.

of lumber. Then they each took off their shoes, stood on the piece of lumber in their bare feet, and rode it down the street. They pretended they were surfing. Dude, they were *sidewalk surfing*. They even adopted surf tricks, such as "hanging five" and "walking the nose." Even in those early days, skaters had style.

The sport grew quickly. The first factory-made board, called the Roller Derby, appeared in the late 1950s. More companies began jumping on the skateboard bandwagon,

and a variety of styles began to appear. The first major techno-
logical advancement came in the early 1960s, when clay wheels
began to replace steel wheels. Not exactly high-tech, but you
have to remember, man had not yet walked on the moon.

Clay wheels gripped the ground better than steel wheels.
But in many ways, they still didn't work too well. If you went
around a turn too fast, the bearings would pop out of the wheels
and scatter on the ground. Hit a pebble, and you skidded. Hit a
rock, and you took flight.

By the mid-1960s, skateboarding had gone national.
Companies such as Makaha and Hobie formed teams and
organized the first skate competitions. They tested riders on
tricks such as freestyle, slalom, nose wheelies, and downhilling.
The competitions featured both boys' and girls' divisions.

In 1973, a surfer named Frank Nasworthy introduced
a skateboard wheel made of a plastic called **urethane.** This
changed the sport forever. Skaters felt a little like their boards
had been given four-wheel drive. Urethane wheels made skating
faster, more fun, quieter, and smoother.

Now, skating was becoming its own sport. And skaters
were developing their own style, different from surfing. That led
to an entirely new skate culture—a world of music, clothes, magazines, and attitude that defined what it meant to be a skater.

Skaters got really creative in the 1970s. In California, a huge drought forced many homeowners to empty their swimming pools. Someone got the idea to try skating in an empty pool. With the new urethane wheels, which are slightly sticky, riders were able to make a sport out of vertical pool skating.

As time went on, skaters began to get air, do **hand plants,** and attempt much more. New tricks were invented practically every day. Skateboard parks were built all over the United States. Skaters who didn't have a pool or a park around began building their own wooden half-pipes. The half-pipes led to even more daring vert moves.

In the 1980s, skate culture became more closely associated with punk music, *Thrasher* magazine, and wild graphics. Superstar skaters such as Tony Hawk, Christian Hosoi, Steve Caballero, Lance Mountain, Mark Gonzales, and Chris Miller began to emerge. Wider and taller half-pipes were built with **PVC,** steel pipe, and concrete lips.

Soon, many skaters began to think that skating had become too cool and too big for its own good. So they got back to basics. In the 1990s, street skating again became popular. Skaters just wanted to walk out their front door and grind the curb, ollie over a fire hydrant, haul down the street, and be **stoked.**

As the decade progressed, the wooden parts known as decks, wheels, and trucks became lighter and tighter. This meant that skaters could take a much more **agro** approach to

As gear improved, skaters could perfect new tricks such as this excellent ollie.

SMOOTH WHEELS

In 1973, a surfer named Frank Nasworthy changed skate history. He was visiting a shop in Purcellville, Virginia, run by the father of a friend of his. One thing his friend's dad sold at his shop was urethane wheels for roller skates. Frank took a few of the wheels home and found that they fit his Hobie skateboard. He couldn't believe how smooth they were compared to clay wheels. Nasworthy began to develop the wheels (called Cadillacs) and promoted them in the San Diego area. At first, skateboarders were reluctant to use "roller rink wheels," but the word spread, and they caught on. Skateboard wheel technology advanced further in 1975, when the first precision bearing wheel came on the market. This ended years of problems with loose ball bearings.

street skating. They began rail sliding (sliding down handrails), soaring down stairs, and ollieing over picnic tables.

At the same time, people were starting to get interested in extreme sports, and skating demonstrations became bigger and flashier. Today, huge stadium shows feature pro skaters on killer half-pipes. They shoot 8 feet (2.4 meters) in the air and perform **gnarly** tricks. The spectacles often include BMX bike riders, motorcycle stunt riders, light shows, and loud music.

Nowadays, in the world of skating, there seems to be something for everyone—street skating, vert skating, skate parks, and downhilling. Skaters can decide which is the most fun for them.

GEAR UP!

When it comes to equipment, skaters are

lucky. All you really need is a board, a helmet, and some pads. (Some communities have laws requiring safety equipment. California, for example, requires skaters under age 18 to wear helmets.) Compared to other sports, skateboarding doesn't cost much. And boards can last for years.

Normally, beginning skaters will buy an inexpensive board from a department store. Then they will put in some

X Games skater Benjamin Bodnar was only 10 when he won the junior world title.

Skaters wear safety gear that includes a helmet and elbow pads.

hours on the board. If they want to get more **core,** they'll visit a skate shop and put together a better board that has longer-lasting parts. These days, many skaters also buy special skateboard shoes. These can be helpful, but they are not necessary.

Here's a list of what you'll need to get started and the approximate price. A typical pro-quality board setup costs $120 to $150.

Deck ($50)

The deck is the wooden part of the board—the part that you stand on. Virtually all decks are made of maple. Maple is a light, strong wood that provides the perfect "snap" for tricks. Choose a deck that fits your size. A longer board with a longer wheelbase is more stable, but a shorter board is more responsive.

Grip Tape ($6)

Grip tape is rough, black tape that goes on top of the deck. It helps your feet grip the board. Grip tape comes in a few different levels of roughness and durability.

Trucks ($20—$50)

Trucks are the pivoting metal parts that hold the wheels to the bottom of the deck. Trucks come in different widths. Pick the width that best suits your deck. Trucks can be tightened by using a wrench or skate tool to adjust a bolt called the king pin. The more you tighten the king pin, the stiffer and more stable the board will ride. Looser trucks make the board more wobbly, but you can **carve** better and lean into your turns more. Typically, beginners keep their trucks tight, and as they get better, they begin to loosen them.

Riser pads ($5)

Riser pads go between the deck and the trucks to add more height to the board. They come in different thicknesses. The

Trucks and wheels come in many forms. Plus, you can decorate your deck however you want!

current trend is *not* to put a riser pad on your board to keep it lighter and lower to the ground for better street performance.

Wheels ($20—$30)

Almost everyone uses urethane wheels. They come in many different sizes. Most skaters use wheels between 2 and 2.5

inches (52 and 63 millimeters) in diameter. A bigger wheel carries more momentum and has a higher top speed. Most pool and vert skaters prefer bigger wheels. Street skaters prefer smaller wheels because they are lighter and faster.

Durometer is the measure of a wheel's hardness. The harder the wheel (101 durometer being the hardest), the faster and more responsive it is. Most skaters who ride in skate parks, in pools, or on ramps use 101 durometer wheels. But if you ride rough streets, drainage ditches, or pitted pools, you'll want 92 to 95 durometer wheels, so that your ride is smoother.

Bearings ($10—$40)

Bearings are round steel balls that are contained within each wheel. The more you pay for them, the faster you'll go. But for a beginner, it's not worth paying for expensive bearings. The ceramic ones are superfast but superexpensive. For most skaters, steel bearings are totally cool.

Helmet ($30—$50)

You should always wear a helmet when you skate. In fact, most skate parks require them. There's a reason: almost all serious skate accidents are head injuries. Don't chance it. The new helmets look cool anyway. Find one that fits snugly.

HALF-PIPES, VERTS, AND MINI RAMPS

Many skateboarders with no access to skate parks or backyard pools build their own half-pipes. Homemade, portable wooden ramps are relatively inexpensive and easy to build. A boring driveway or an empty parking lot can be quickly transformed into a rad playground with just a few ramps. Working with an adult, you can make these ramps using common household tools and materials purchased at a local home shop. For free instructions on how to make your own ramps, go to: *www.heckler.com/ramps/halfpiphi.html* or *www.rickdahlen.com/hpplans/ plans.html*. For more involved instructions that you have to pay for, visit *http://skatoramps.com*.

Knee, wrist, and elbow pads ($15—$20 each, $50 for an entire set)

These pads are also very important. They provide a level of safety that allows a skater to get rad without worrying about getting scrapes, or worse. Some have zippers, some have Velcro. All the top pro skaters wear pads.

Shoes ($40—$100)

Skating eats shoes. You can find durable leather, nylon, and cloth skate shoes in skate shops and some department stores and shoe shops. The best have reinforced or padded soles so you don't bruise your heel coming down from ollies and airs. Beware: the most durable shoes can take a while to break in.

Once you have a board and saftey gear,

find a smooth, relatively flat area to begin skating. Don't choose a busy street where there is danger of the board—or you—zinging out into traffic. Many people begin in their garage, but an empty parking lot or basketball court will do.

Next, you must determine if you are "goofy." In skating, this has nothing to do with your personality. In fact, a lot of the best skaters are really goofy! Riding goofy means riding with

This skater is riding "regular" with his left foot in front of his right on the board.

your right foot forward on the board. Riding "regular" is with your left foot forward. Choose whichever feels most comfortable and stick with it.

Begin by learning how to push the board forward. Most skaters begin by pushing off with their back foot, while their front foot stays planted mid-board. Some people also learn to kick with their front foot. This is called "kicking mongo." Learning to kick both ways is rad because on long skateboard excursions, if one leg gets tired, you can switch to the other. To stop, put either one of your feet down and drag it on the ground. Or jump off.

Learn to do a carve turn—where the wheels don't come off the ground. To turn, put your weight on your front foot and turn your shoulders whichever way you want to go. Your body and the board will follow. You can do a "tic-tac" turn by putting your weight on your back foot, then lifting the nose of the board and tapping it to either side. You can also use a rapid tic-tac motion to generate speed.

Then start doing slides. Get going fast and, instead of carving or lifting the front of the board to turn, lift your weight slightly off the board and let it slide around. You can slide 180 degrees and go backward. As you improve, make sure to get used to going fast, because most tricks in parks or half-pipes require a lot of speed.

Visit skate parks or half-pipes to see what other skaters are doing. You can watch videos to get tips, too. As you get better, the tricks will become easier and easier. You'll also begin to develop your own style and maybe even begin making up your own tricks. Some basic tricks are:

Bomb Drop

Ride straight off something—curbs, benches, planters—and drop straight to the ground.

Nose Wheelie Invented way back in the 1950s. Take your weight off the back of your board and balance on your front wheels as you glide.

Simply leaning your body in the direction you want to turn is the easiest way to guide your board.

This skater performs a perfect tail grind on a rail during a skate park competition.

The Manual A wheelie on your back wheel. Like popping a wheelie on your bike.

Curb Grind Ride the curb so that your outside back wheel drops over the edge and you are grinding on your axle.

After learning these tricks, most skateboarders move on to the ollie, which is the basis of most advanced vert and street skating. When the ollie has been mastered, the tricks take off.

In these days of extreme sports, skateboarding has become more and more rad, both on the streets and on the big vert ramps. Skate pioneer Tony Hawk has developed a huge repertoire of vert tricks, including what he calls a 900. In this trick, he skates to the top of the ramp and launches himself into the air. Then he turns his body two and a half times in midair, and comes back down.

Skateboarding tricks are endless. There are different hand plants, aerials, kick flips, **varials,** and more. Some skaters even switch from regular to goofy in mid-ride. There is only one requirement to getting more advanced: board time. It's like anything: the more time you spend doing it, the better you get.

THE OLLIE

The ollie is the skater's way of taking flight. Once you learn it, a whole new world of tricks opens up. It's a way of getting air on flat land. Alan Gelfand, a pro skater from Florida, invented the ollie when he was just 13. Gelfand named the trick after his own nickname, Ollie.

To do the ollie, position the ball of one foot on the back lip of the board and the other foot directly behind the front truck of the board, and bend your knees. As you roll, quickly extend your back leg, pushing your tail down, and popping it against the ground.

As the board lifts up into the air, drag your front foot up the board until it is at the nose. Push your front foot forward and pull your back foot up to allow the board to level out. Now you are in midair. Let your legs straighten, and then bend them as you hit the ground to soften your landing.

STARS AND COMPETITION

The sport of skateboarding has been

changed forever by huge extreme sport stadium shows such as ESPN's X Games. In these shows, difficulty of tricks is often valued higher than *soul skating*—skating that is done for personal expression. These skate demonstrations and contests are accompanied by loud music, flashing lights, and bellowing announcers. Many events also feature popular rock bands.

In these contests, more is better—more revolutions, more height, more difficulty. Contestants typically get 45 seconds to show what they can do. A skater jumps into the vert ramp and shows off his latest tricks.

The main skate contest in the United States is the Tampa Pro. The contest features both street and vert competitions. In 2003, the same year he was named Skater of the Year by *Thrasher* magazine, Tony Trujillo won the event. Trujillo is among a new generation of skaters who combine **old school** style with new generation tricks. The fact that Trujillo won the Tampa Pro shows that skateboarding judges are getting more **chill.** They once again value style and personality as much as pure technique.

One of the most remarkable performances in the 2003 Tampa Pro came from Ryan Sheckler. Even though Ryan is only

Ryan Sheckler, only 13, stunned the skating world with his awesome performances in top pro events.

13 years old, he finished fourth overall in the contest. Ryan began skating when he was only three years old. He got some help along the way from one of his older friends. Tony Hawk bought him a ramp when Ryan was just six years old.

Some of the other main events each year in the United States include the Slam City Jam and the ever popular X Games. There are also traveling skate demonstrations, such as

Tony Hawk's Boom Boom HuckJam, the Vans Pleased to Meet

You Tour, the Warped Tour, the Core Tour, and the Skateboarder

Road Tour.

Some of the most respected skaters in the world now

refuse to do competitions. They believe that the big events

compromise the true spirit of skating. The most famous of these

skaters is Chad Muska. Muska has attracted sponsorships from

companies such as Shorty's and Ghetto Child just for getting his pictures in magazines, releasing his own videos, selling his own rap album, and appearing at **demos.**

Girl skaters are becoming more and more common in skate parks and bowls around the country. The All Girl Skate Jam now tours the country every year, with 20 pro girls and 50 to 100 local girls showing up to skate each event. There are special girl skateboarder Web sites, and a new girls' skate company named Burly Girls. The best skaters include Cara-Beth Burnside, who has been competing in vert competitions since 1991 and is also a professional snowboarder. Elissa Steamer of Fort Myers, Florida, is the first girl to have a pro model street board with her name on it. She is considered an outstanding street skater. In the 2003 Tampa Pro, she skated against the boys.

Skateboarding is now at a crossroads. It's still rooted in youthful rebellion. But lately, board companies and media outlets have made it very mainstream. For instance, NBC launched a television series in October 2003 called *Skate.* The show follows the life of a fictional skater named Josh Raden as he attempts to go pro.

Skate culture continues to evolve. Many skaters think of themselves as part of a larger sports movement that includes surfing and snowboarding. Some skaters like metal music, some like jazz, some like old school rock. The variety is endless, and it stimulates the sport. The next 10 years will see further mixing of vert, street, and backyard pool skating. Few people

Simply the best: Tony Hawk has invented or perfected more tricks than any skater in history.

HOW HAWK TOOK FLIGHT

Tony Hawk is the most famous skater of all time. But when Tony was a kid, he had problems concentrating and difficulties in school. His parents took him to a psychologist because he was so hard on himself when he couldn't do things. The psychologist said he was gifted and advised his parents to put him in advanced classes. When he was nine, his brother gave him a learning tool that the school and the experts never thought of: a skateboard.

Skating focused his hyperactive mind and tapped his boundless energy. By 12, Hawk was sponsored by Dogtown Skateboards; by 14, he was pro. By 16, Hawk was the best skateboarder in the world.

Even though he doesn't compete any longer, at age 35 he's still hyperactive. He now owns his own clothing company and wrote a best-selling autobiography, *Hawk—Occupation: Skateboarder.* He helped create Tony Hawk's Pro Skater and Pro Skater 2 games for Playstation.

Skating provided a way for Hawk to focus himself, and now he gives a lot back to the sport that gave him so much. His foundation spends $400,000 each year helping to establish skate parks all over the country.

do just one type of skating now. More and more kids embrace all aspects of skating. In doing so, they have become part of a worldwide network of friends—a core group of skaters.

The most important aspect of skating, though, remains its individuality. At its most basic, it is still a sport where skaters make their own rules. Each skater gets on the board, goes out in the street, and skates. That will never change.

GLOSSARY

aerials —Also called airs and getting air; tricks in which you leave the ground.

agro —Short for *aggressive;* to approach skating, or life, in an aggressive way.

carve —Turn.

chill —Mellow, cool, easy to get along with.

core —Short for *hardcore;* completely dedicated to skateboarding.

demos —Skateboarding demonstrations with no competitive element.

gnarly —Difficult, crazy, or just plain stupid.

half-pipe —A U-shaped ramp of any size, usually with a flat area in the middle.

hand plants —Skaters put one hand down on the ground or on the lip of a half-pipe, usually while they are doing a trick.

kick flips —Ollies in which the boards rotate in midair, completely flipping over and then land on the wheels again.

old school —Something that became popular 10 or more years ago.

pvc —An abbreviation that stands for polyvinyl chloride, the name for a common thermo-plastic resin used in many manufactured products including half-pipes.

rad —Short for *radical;* impressive, extreme.

rip —A slang term that means to go all out, to get out there on your board and do your thing.

stoked —Feeling good, enthusiastic and happy about something.

urethane —Type of plastic used to make skateboard wheels; it is sturdy and slightly sticky and comes in a wide variety of colors.

varials —Ollies in which the boards spin 180 degrees in the air, so that the backs of the boards are facing forward when they land.

vert —Short for *vertical.*

FIND OUT MORE

Museums

SKATOPIA
34961 Hutton Road
Rutland, OH 45775
740/742-1110
Skatopia is an 88-acre (36-hectare) farm that has an enormous collection of skateboards, a huge indoor wooden bowl, and countless ramps.

SKATELAB
4226 Valley Fair Street
Simi Valley, CA 93063
805/578-0040
Skatelab has a huge collection of skateboard products and memorabilia. Also on display are really cool scooters from the 1930s. A 15,000-square foot (1,394-square meter) skate park sits next to the museum.

On the Web

Visit our home page for lots of links about skateboarding:
http://www.childsworld.com/links.html

NOTE TO PARENTS, TEACHERS, AND LIBRARIANS: We routinely check our Web links to make sure they're safe, active sites—so encourage your readers to check them out!

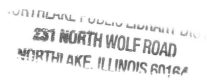

Books

Bermudez, Ben. *Skate! The Mongo's Guide to Skateboarding.* New York: 17th Street Productions, 2001.

Hawk, Tony. *Hawk—Occupation: Skateboarder.* New York: ReganBooks, 2000.

Thatcher, Kevin. *Thrasher Presents How to Build Skateboard Ramps: Half-pipes, Boxes, Bowls, and More.* New York: Random House, 1992.

Werner, Doug, and Steve Badillo. *Skateboarder's Start-Up: A Beginner's Guide to Skateboarding.* San Diego: Tracks Publishing, 2000.

INDEX

About the Author

Russ Spencer is a Southern California writer, film-maker, and surfer. His articles have appeared in many publications including *Outside*, the *Surfer's Journal*, the *New York Times* Sunday magazine, *Utne Reader*, and the *Los Angeles Times*.